My First French Book

KINGFISHER

KINGFISHER

First published 2007 by Kingfisher
an imprint of Macmillan Children's Books
a division of Macmillan Publishers Limited
20 New Wharf Road, London N1 9RR
Basingstoke and Oxford
Associated companies throughout the world
www.panmacmillan.com

ISBN 978 0 7534 1387 6

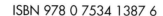

10 11 12 13 14 15
10TR/0211/WKT/PICA(PICA)/140MA/C

Printed in China

Suggestions for parents

Sharing this book with your child is the ideal way to help him or her start the enjoyable journey of learning a foreign language. This bright, appealing book will establish the skills needed for confident learning and will act as an invaluable prompt for reading and becoming familiar with words in both English and French.

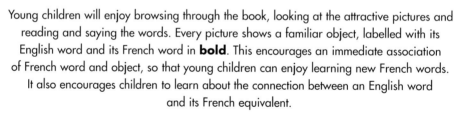

Young children will enjoy browsing through the book, looking at the attractive pictures and reading and saying the words. Every picture shows a familiar object, labelled with its English word and its French word in **bold**. This encourages an immediate association of French word and object, so that young children can enjoy learning new French words. It also encourages children to learn about the connection between an English word and its French equivalent.

In French, nouns (words for objects) are masculine or feminine. Instead of one word for 'the', as in English, French uses **le** for masculine nouns and **la** for feminine nouns. Or **l'** is used if the word comes before a vowel, whether it is masculine or feminine. **Le, la** and **l'** are singular, used if there is only one object. **Les** is plural, used if there is more than one object.

At the end of the book is a complete alphabetical list of all the French words included in *My First French Book*, along with a guide to how to say each word and some general hints about French pronunciation.

Contents

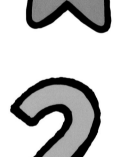

Numbers 1 to 10
Les nombres de 1 à 10

1 one
un / une

2 two
deux

3 three
trois

4 four
quatre

5 five
cinq

6 six
six

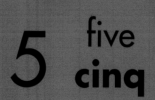

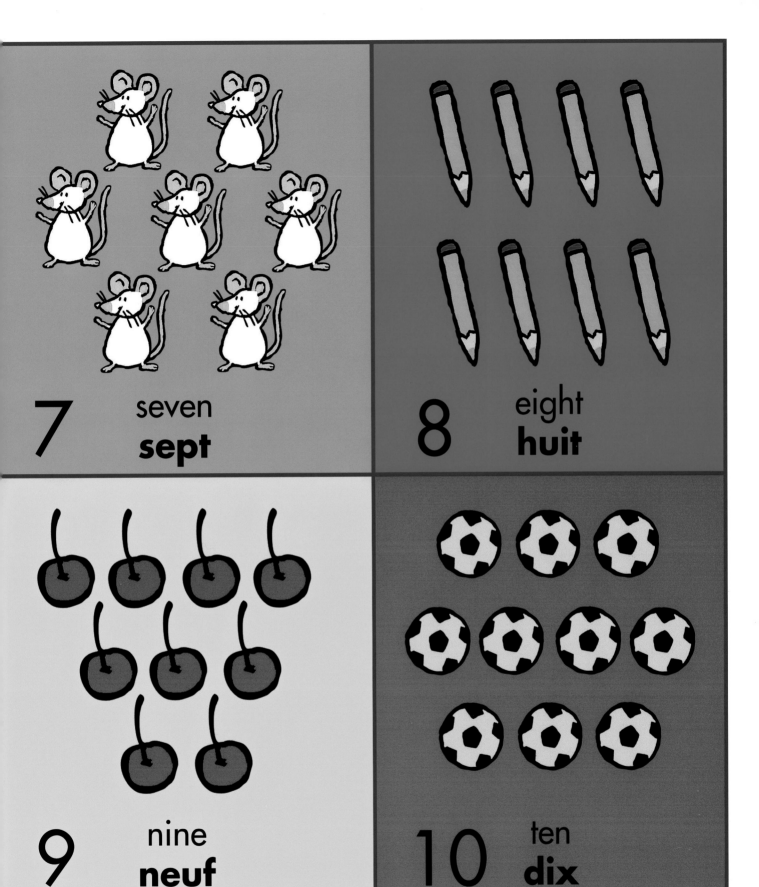

7 seven **sept**

8 eight **huit**

9 nine **neuf**

10 ten **dix**

Numbers 11 to 20
Les nombres de 11 à 20

11 eleven **onze**

12 twelve **douze**

13 thirteen **treize**

14 fourteen **quatorze**

15 fifteen **quinze**

16 sixteen **seize**

17 seventeen
dix-sept

18 eighteen
dix-huit

19 nineteen
dix-neuf

20 twenty
vingt

More numbers
Plus de nombres

30

thirty
trente

40

forty
quarante

50

fifty
cinquante

60

sixty
soixante

70

seventy
soixante-dix

80

eighty
quatre-vingts

90

ninety
quatre-vingt-dix

100

one hundred
cent

Colours **Les couleurs**

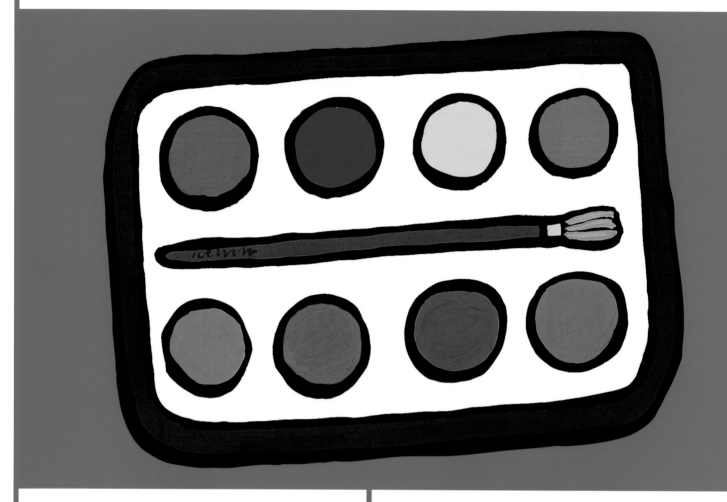

black
noir

white
blanc

red
rouge

blue
bleu

yellow
jaune

purple
violet

green
vert

orange
orange

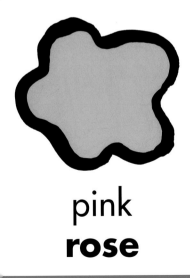

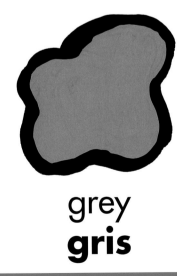

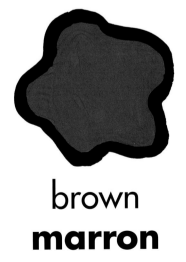

pink
rose

grey
gris

brown
marron

Shapes **Les formes**

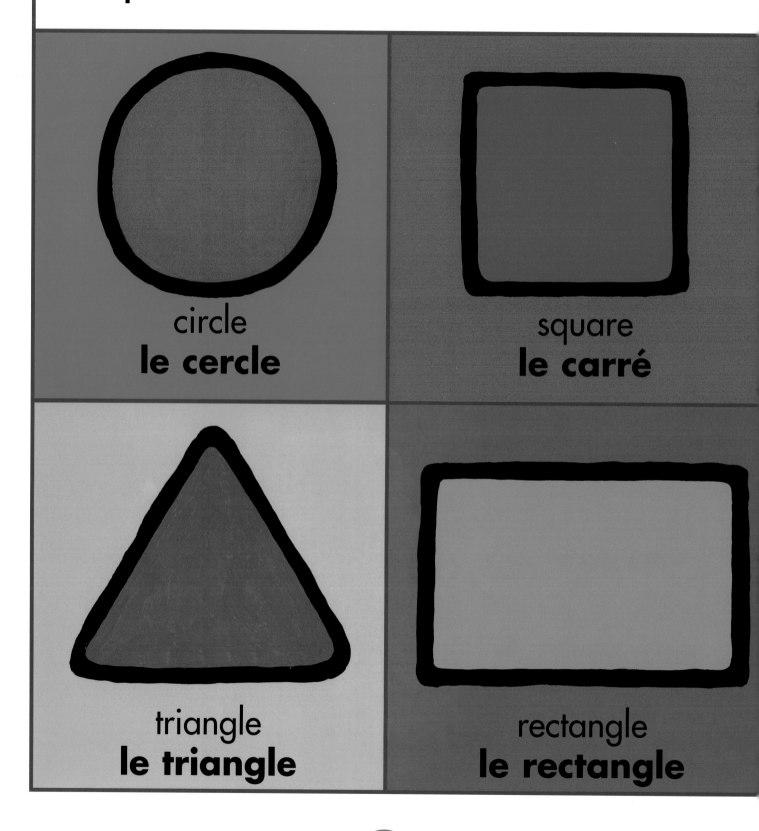

circle
le cercle

square
le carré

triangle
le triangle

rectangle
le rectangle

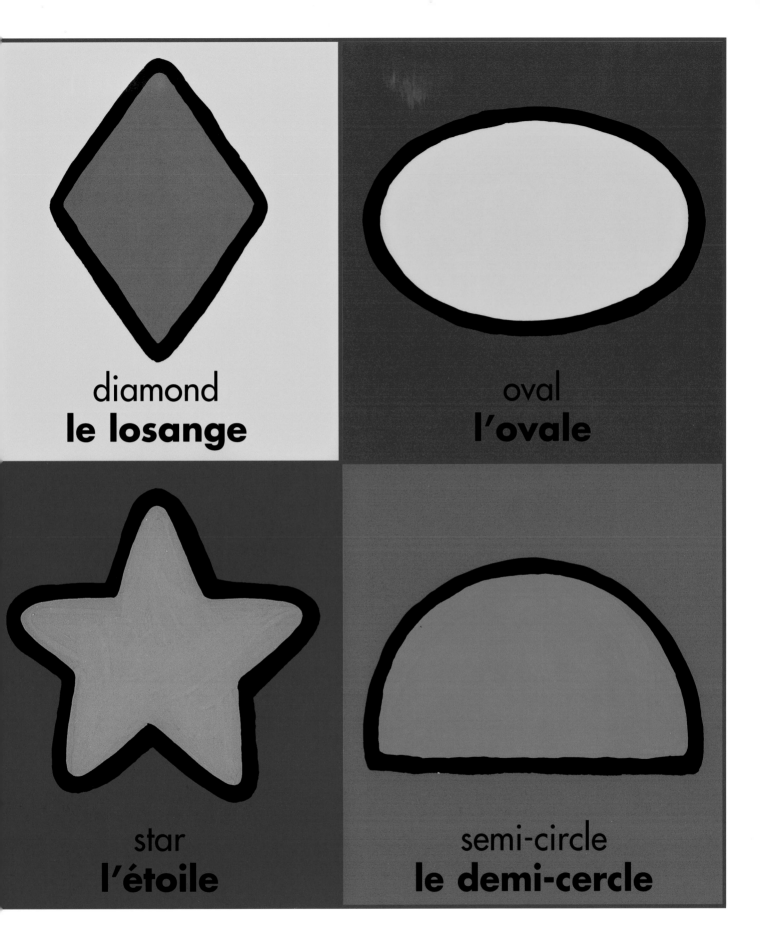

diamond
le losange

oval
l'ovale

star
l'étoile

semi-circle
le demi-cercle

Clothes **Les vêtements**

T-shirt
le tee-shirt

skirt
la jupe

gloves
les gants

jeans
le jean

socks
les chaussettes

14

coat
le manteau

trainers
les baskets

jumper
le pull

shoes
les chaussures

belt
la ceinture

cap
la casquette

scarf
l'écharpe

The body **Le corps**

nose
le nez

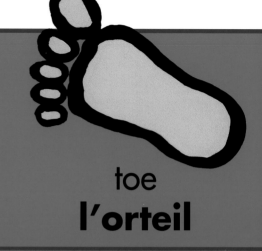

toe
l'orteil

back
le dos

chin
le menton

ear
l'oreille

hair
les cheveux

foot
le pied

hand
la main

eye
l'oeil

arm
le bras

leg
la jambe

knee
le genou

17

Food **La nourriture**

pineapple
l'ananas

bread
le pain

banana
la banane

strawberry
la fraise

egg
l'oeuf

pie
la tourte

carrot
la carotte

ham
le jambon

cheese
le fromage

orange
l'orange

apple
la pomme

ice lolly
la glace

The bedroom **La chambre**

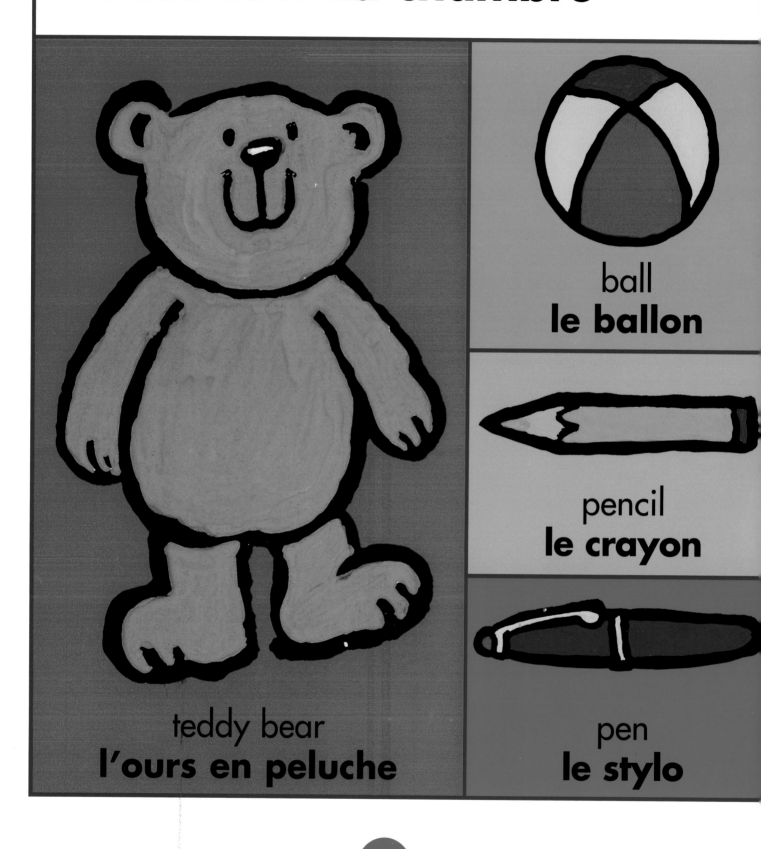

teddy bear
l'ours en peluche

ball
le ballon

pencil
le crayon

pen
le stylo

bed
le lit

lamp
la lampe

yo-yo
le yo-yo

carpet
le tapis

comb
le peigne

doll
la poupée

book
le livre

kite
le cerf-volant

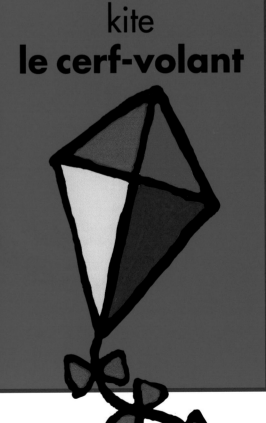

The kitchen **La cuisine**

fork
la fourchette

knife
le couteau

spoon
la cuillère

bowl
le bol

plate
l'assiette

jar
le pot de verre

cooker
la cuisinière

apron
le tablier

frying pan
la poêle

cup
la tasse

The bathroom **La salle de bains**

bath
la baignoire

duck
le canard

sponge
l'éponge

towel
la serviette

24

basin
le lavabo

door
la porte

mirror
le miroir

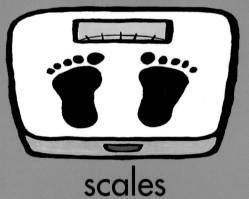

scales
la balance

toothpaste
le dentifrice

soap
le savon

toothbrush
la brosse à dents

The garden **Le jardin**

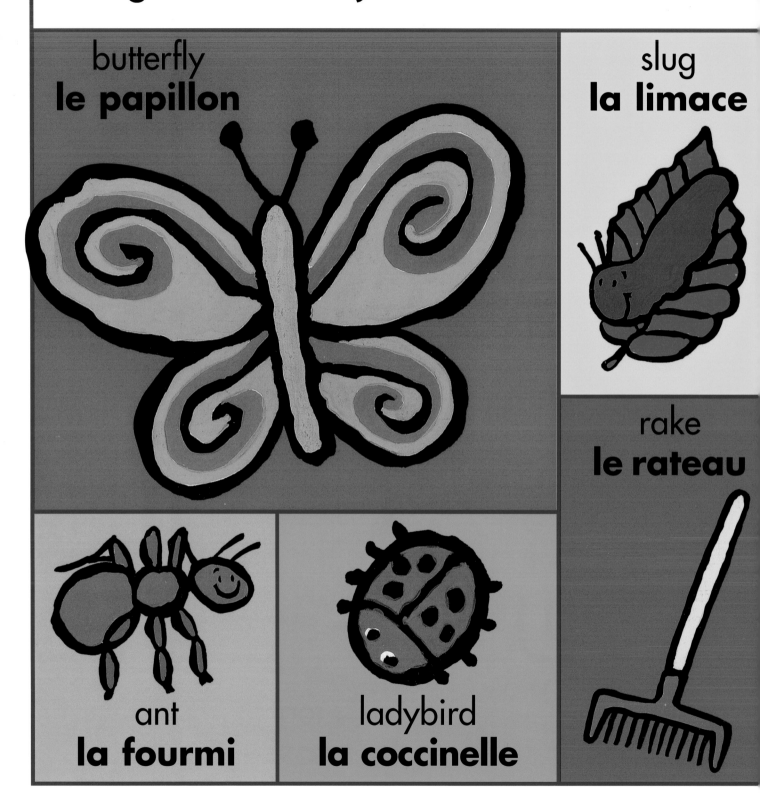

butterfly
le papillon

slug
la limace

rake
le rateau

ant
la fourmi

ladybird
la coccinelle

bird
l'oiseau

gate
la portail

spider's web
la toile d'araignée

leaf
la feuille

nest
le nid

frog
la grenouille

worm
le ver
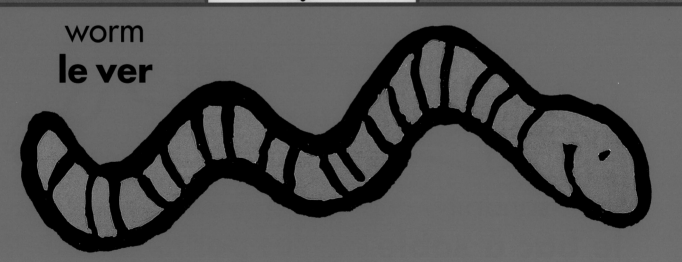

27

The park **Le parc**

pushchair
la poussette

dog
le chien

rollerblades
les patins à roulette

sandpit
le bac à sable

28

flower
la fleur

pond
la mare

swing
la balançoire

tricycle
le tricycle

tree
l'arbre

slide
le toboggan

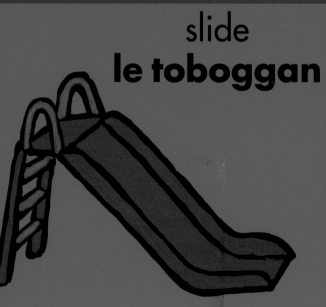

see-saw
la bascule

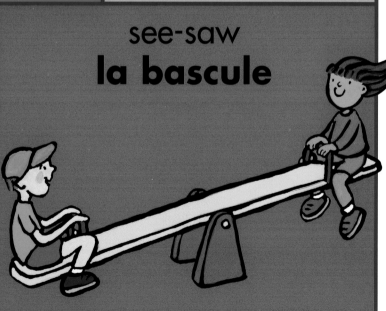

School **L'école**

teacher
la maîtresse

table
la table

paint
la peinture

paintbrush
le pinceau

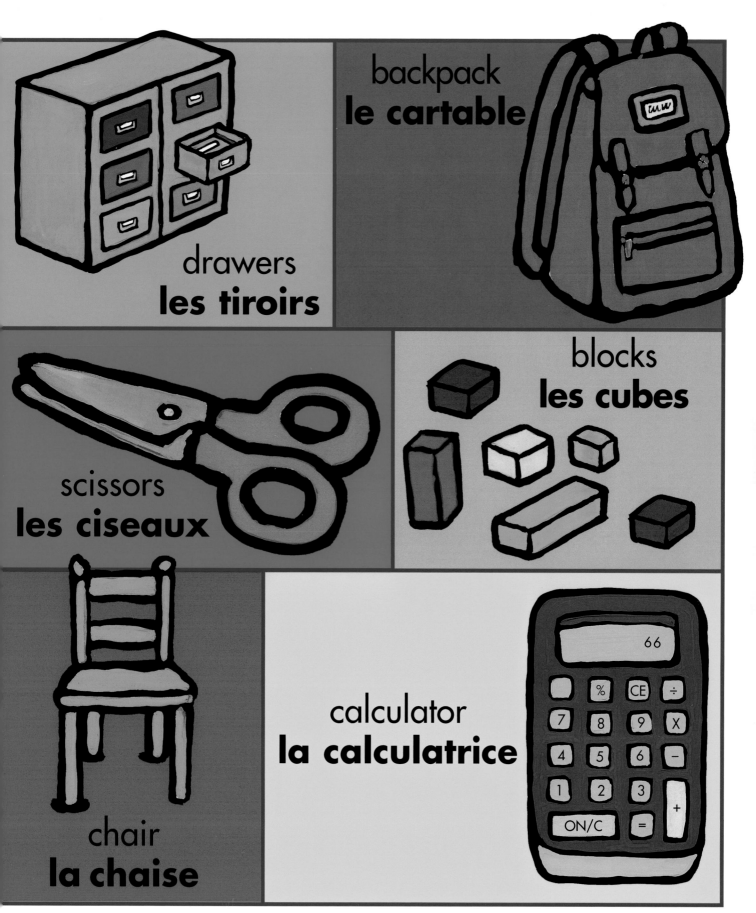

drawers
les tiroirs

backpack
le cartable

scissors
les ciseaux

blocks
les cubes

chair
la chaise

calculator
la calculatrice

The supermarket **Le supermarché**

assistant
la vendeuse

milk
le lait

jam
la confiture

trolley
le chariot

vegetables
les légumes

can
la boîte de conserve

box
la boîte

bag
le sac

till
la caisse

fruit juice
le jus de fruit

purse
le porte-monnaie

money
l'argent

The seaside **La plage**

starfish
l'étoile de mer

sea
la mer

sandals
les sandales

fish
le poisson

yacht
le voilier

crab
le crabe

sandcastle
le château de sable

spade
la pelle

fishing net
l'épuisette

bucket
le seau

shell
le coquillage

The farm **La ferme**

tractor
le tracteur

goat
la chèvre

barn
la grange

pig
le cochon

bull
le taureau

36

house
la maison

chick
le poussin

farmer
le fermier

calf
le veau

sheep
le mouton

cow
la vache

cat
le chat

Animals **Les animaux**

tiger
le tigre

wolf
le loup

swan
le cygne

deer
le cerf

monkey
le singe

parrot
le perroquet

bear
l'ours

fox
le renard

elephant
l'éléphant

seal
le phoque

toucan
le toucan

zebra
le zèbre

People **Les gens**

woman
la femme

girl
la fille

man
l'homme

boy
le garçon

baby
le bébé

vet
le vétérinaire

chef
le chef

dancer
la danseuse

spy
l'espion

dentist
le dentiste

clown
le clown

nurse
l'infirmière

Transport **Le transport**

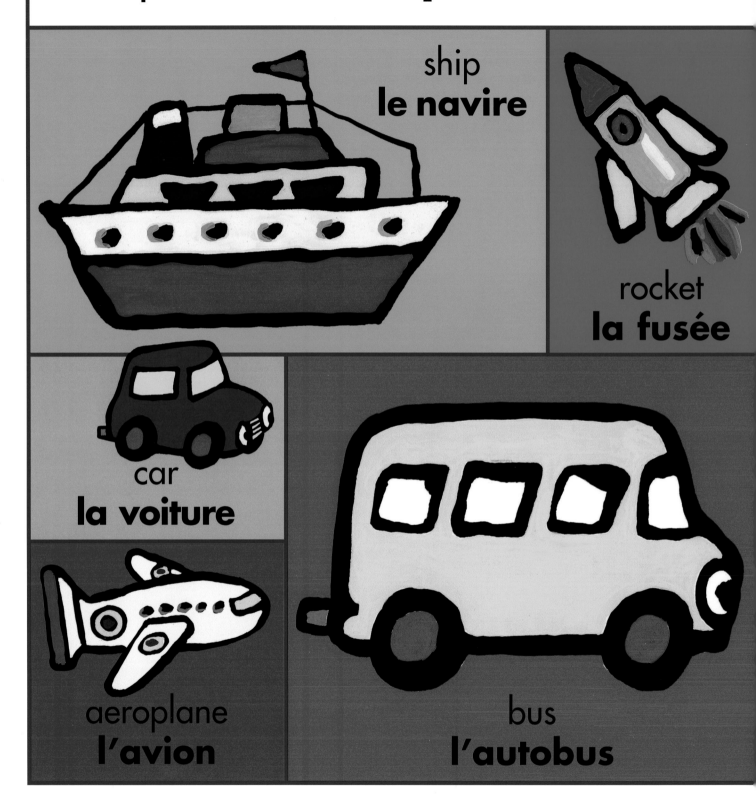

ship
le navire

rocket
la fusée

car
la voiture

aeroplane
l'avion

bus
l'autobus

bicycle
la bicyclette

boat
le bateau

lorry
le camion

motorbike
la moto

train
le train

The weather **Le temps**

sun
le soleil

hail
la grêle

lightning
l'éclair

fog
le brouillard

rain
la pluie

ice
la glace

snow
la neige

moon
la lune

cloud
le nuage

wind
le vent

storm
l'orage

Word list

In this list you will find all the French words in this book, in **bold**. Next to each one is a guide to pronunciation (how to say it) and the English translation.

Remember that in French, nouns (words for objects) are masculine or feminine. Instead of one word for 'the', as in English, French uses **le** for masculine nouns and **la** for feminine nouns. Or **l'** is used if the word comes before a vowel, whether it is masculine or feminine. **Le, la** and **l'** are singular, used if there is only one object. **Les** is plural, used if there is more than one object.

Some pronunciation tips

When following the pronunciation guide, read the guide words as if they are English words. Some letter sounds are different from how you would read them in English, though, as follows:

● When you see 'g' in the pronunciation guide, say it like the 'g' in 'garden', not like the 'g' in 'gentle'.

● When you see the letter 'j' in the pronunciation guide, you should say it softly, like the 's' sound in the English word 'pleasure'.

● When you see the letter 'n' at the end of a word, make the sound at the back of your nose. There is no sound exactly like it in English.

● Make the 'r' sound by slightly growling at the back of your throat.

abc

l'ananas (la-na-na)	pineapple
les animaux (lays a-nee-moe)	animals
l'arbre (lar-br)	tree
l'argent (lar-jon)	money
l'assiette (lass-yett)	plate
l'autobus (lo-toe-bews)	bus
l'avion (lav-yon)	aeroplane
le bac à sable (le bac a sah-bl)	sandpit
la baignoire (la ban-ywar)	bath
la balance (la ba-lans)	scales
la balançoire (la ba-lan-swar)	swing
le ballon (le ba-lon)	ball
la banane (la ba-nan)	banana
la bascule (la bass-kewl)	see-saw
les baskets (lay bas-ketts)	trainers
le bateau (le ba-toe)	boat
le bébé (le bay-bay)	baby
la bicyclette (la bee-see-klett)	bicycle
blanc (blon)	white
bleu (bler)	blue
la boîte (la bwat)	box
la boîte de conserve (la bwat de kon-sairv)	tin
le bol (le bol)	bowl
le bras (le bra)	arm
la brosse à dents (la bross a don)	toothbrush
le brouillard (le brwee-yar)	fog
la caisse (la kess)	till
la calculatrice (la kal-koo-la-treess)	calculator
le camion (le ka-mee-on)	lorry
le canard (le ka-nar)	duck
le carré (le ka-rray)	square
la carotte (la ka-rrott)	carrot
le cartable (le kar-tah-bl)	backpack
la casquette (la kass-kett)	cap
la ceinture (la sain-tewr)	belt
cent (son)	a hundred
le cercle (le sair-kle)	circle
le cerf (le sairf)	deer
le cerf-volant (le sairf-vo-lon)	kite
la chaise (la shayz)	chair
la chambre (la shom-br)	bedroom
le chariot (le sha-rio)	trolley
le chat (le sha)	cat
le château de sable (le sha-toe de sah-bl)	sandcastle
les chaussettes (lay show-sett)	socks
les chaussures (lay show-sewr)	shoes
le chef (le shef)	chef
les cheveux (lay sher-ver)	hair
la chèvre (la shevr)	goat
le chien (le shee-an)	dog
cinq (sank)	five
cinquante (san-kont)	fifty
les ciseaux (lay si-zoh)	scissors
le clown (le clown)	clown

la coccinelle (la ko-ksee-nell)	ladybird
le cochon (le kosh-on)	pig
la confiture (la kon-fee-tewr)	jam
le coquillage (le ko-kee-yaj)	shell
le corps (le kor)	body
les couleurs (lay coo-lewr)	colours
le couteau (le koo-toe)	knife
le crabe (le krab)	crab
le crayon (le kray-on)	pencil
les cubes (lay koob)	blocks
la cuillère (la kwee-yair)	spoon
la cuisine (la kwee-zeen)	kitchen
la cuisinière (la kwee-zee-nyair)	cooker
le cygne (le seen-ye)	swan

def

la danseuse (la don-serz)	dancer
le demi-cercle (le de-mee-sair-kle)	semi-circle
le dentifrice (le don-tee-freess)	toothpaste
le dentiste (le don-teest)	dentist
deux (der)	two
dix (dees)	ten
dix-huit (deess-weet)	eighteen
dix-neuf (deess-neuf)	nineteen
dix-sept (deess-sett)	seventeen
le dos (le doh)	back
douze (dooz)	twelve

l'écharpe (lay-sharp)	scarf
l'éclair (lay-clair)	lightning
l'école (lay-kole)	school
l'éléphant (lay-lay-fon)	elephant
l'éponge (lay-ponj)	sponge
l'épuisette (lay-pwee-sett)	fishing net
l'espion (less-pee-on)	spy
l'étoile (lay-twahl)	star
l'étoile de mer (lay-twahl de mair)	starfish

la femme (la fam)	woman
la feuille (la foy-ye)	leaf
la ferme (la fairm)	farm
le fermier (le fair-mee-ay)	farmer
la fille (la fee-ye)	girl
la fleur (la fler)	flower
les formes (lay forrme)	shapes
la fourchette (la four-shett)	fork
la fourmi (la four-mee)	ant
la fraise (la fraiz)	strawberry
le fromage (le fro-mahj)	cheese
la fusée (la fooz-ay)	rocket

ghi

les gants (lay gon)	gloves
le garçon (le gar-sonn)	boy
le genou (le je-noo)	knee
les gens (lay jon)	people

la glace (la glass)	ice or ice cream
la grange (la gronj)	barn
la grêle (la grail)	hail
la grenouille (la gre-nweey)	frog
gris (gree)	grey

l'homme (lom)	man
huit (weet)	eight

l'infirmière (lan-fer-myair)	nurse

jkl

la jambe (la jomb)	leg
le jambon (le jom-bon)	ham
le jardin (le jar-dan)	garden
jaune (jone)	yellow
le jean (le jean)	jeans
la jupe (la joop)	skirt
le jus de fruit (le juz de frwee)	fruit juice

le lait (le lay)	milk
la lampe (la lomp)	lamp
le lavabo (le la-va-bo)	basin
les légumes (lay lay-goom)	vegetables
la limace (la lee-mass)	slug
le lit (le lee)	bed
le livre (le leevr)	book
le losange (le lo-zanj)	diamond
le loup (le loo)	wolf
la lune (la loon)	moon

mn

la main (la man)	hand
la maison (la may-zon)	house
la maîtresse (la may-tress)	teacher (primary school)
le manteau (le mon-toe)	coat
la mare (la mahrr)	pond
marron (ma-rron)	brown
le menton (le men-ton)	chin
la mer (la mer)	sea
le miroir (le mee-rwar)	mirror
la moto (la mo-toe)	motorbike
le mouton (le moo-ton)	sheep

le navire (le na-veer-e)	ship
la neige (la nej)	snow
neuf (nerf)	nine
le nez (le nez)	nose
le nid (le nee)	nest
noir (nwar)	black
les nombres (lay nom-br)	numbers
la nourriture (la nou-rree-tewr)	food
le nuage (le new-ahj)	cloud

op

l'oeil (loy)	eye
l'oeuf (lerf)	egg
l'oiseau (lwa-zoh)	bird
l'orage (lor-ahj)	storm
orange (or-onj)	orange (colour)
l'orange (lor-onj)	orange (fruit)
l'oreille (lor-ay)	ear
l'orteil (lor-tay)	toe
onze (onz)	eleven
l'ours (loorss)	bear
l'ours en peluche (loorss on pe-loosh)	teddy bear
l'ovale (lo-vahl)	oval
le pain (le pan)	bread
le papillon (le pa-pee-yon)	butterfly
le parc (le park)	park
les patins à roulette (lay pa-tan a roo-lett)	rollerblades
le peigne (le payn-ye)	comb
la peinture (la payn-tewr)	paints
la pelle (la pell)	spade
le perroquet (le per-ro-kay)	parrot
le phoque (le fock)	seal
le pied (le pee-ay)	foot
le pinceau (le pan-sow)	paintbrush
la plage (la plaj)	beach
la pluie (la ploo-ee)	rain
la poêle (la po-ayl)	frying pan
le poisson (le pwa-sonn)	fish
la pomme (la pomm)	apple
le portail (le por-ta-ye)	gate
la porte (la por-te)	door
le porte-monnaie (le port-mo-nay)	purse
le pot de verre (le po de verr)	jar
la poupée (la poo-pay)	doll
la poussette (la poo-sett)	pushchair
le poussin (le poo-san)	chick
le pull (le pewl)	jumper

qrs

quarante (ka-ront)	forty
quatorze (ka-torz)	fourteen
quatre (katr)	four
quatre-vingt-dix (katr-van-deess)	ninety
quatre-vingts (katr-van)	eighty
quinze (kanz)	fifteen
le rateau (le ra-tow)	rake
le rectangle (le rek-tongl)	rectangle
le renard (le re-nar)	fox
rose (rose)	pink
rouge (rooj)	red
le sac (le sac)	bag
la salle de bains (la sall de ban)	bathroom
les sandales (lay san-dahl)	sandals
le savon (le sa-von)	soap

le seau (le soh)	bucket
seize (sehz)	sixteen
sept (set)	seven
la serviette (la sair-vee-ett)	towel
le singe (le sanj)	monkey
six (seess)	six
le soleil (le so-lay)	sun
soixante (swa-zont)	sixty
soixante-dix (swa-zont dees)	seventy
le stylo (le stee-lo)	pen
le supermarché (le soo-per-mar-shay)	supermarket

tu

la table (la tah-bl)	table
le tablier (le ta-blee-ay)	apron
le tapis (le ta-pee)	carpet
la tasse (la tass)	cup
le taureau (le toor-oh)	bull
le tee-shirt (le tee-shirt)	T-shirt
le temps (le tom)	weather
le tigre (le tee-gr)	tiger
les tiroirs (lay teer-wahr)	drawers
le toboggan (le to-bog-gan)	slide
la toile d'araignée (la twal da-ray-nyay)	spider's web
le toucan (le too-kan)	toucan
la tourte (la toor-te)	pie
le tracteur (le trak-ter)	tractor
le train (le tran)	train
le transport (le tran-spor)	transport
treize (trehz)	thirteen
trente (tront)	thirty
le triangle (le tre-ongl)	triangle
le tricycle (le tree-see-kl)	tricycle
trois (trwa)	three
un or **une** (an or oon)	one

vw

la vache (la vash)	cow
le veau (le voh)	calf
la vendeuse (la von-derz)	assistant (in a shop)
le vent (le von)	wind
le ver (le vair)	worm
vert (vair)	green
les vêtements (lay vett-mon)	clothes
le vétérinaire (le vay-tayr-e-nair)	vet
vingt (van)	twenty
violet (vee-o-lay)	purple
le voilier (le vwa-lee-ay)	yacht
la voiture (la vwa-toor)	car

xyz

le yo-yo (le yo-yo)	yo-yo
le zèbre (le zehbr)	zebra